Walking The Road Of Grief
A Journey I Never Wanted To Take

Judy Proffitt

This I recall to my mind, therefore have I hope.
It is of the Lord's mercies that we are not consumed,
because his compassions fail not. They are new every
morning: great is thy faithfulness. The Lord is my
portion, saith my soul; therefore will I hope in him.
The Lord is good unto them that wait for him, to the
soul that seeketh him. It is good that a man should both
hope and quietly wait for the salvation of the Lord.

Lamentations 3:21-26

These poems were written in the days and months
following the death of my husband, Robert.
He died December 31, 2023, just two months short of
what would have been the sixty-third Anniversary of
our marriage.

If you have lost someone you loved deeply, I am sure
you have experienced many of these feelings. I have
left the date when they were written; as you can see,
time does not lessen the feelings of loss.

I wrote these poems as my way of expressing the grief
that I have from losing the love of my life,
and as a tribute to him for the loving husband
and father he was.

I pray that they will help others acknowledge and
express their grief in some small way and find comfort
and hope in God's eternal promises.

Judy Proffitt

January

*Yea though I walk through the
valley of the shadow of death,
I will fear no evil,
for Thou art with me.*

Psalm 23:4

ROBERT

When Robert went to Heaven from Hospice,
I had to go back home alone.
When I opened the door and entered,
The Silence screamed, "This will never be home."

Then I went down the hall to the bedroom,
The bed looked twenty feet wide.
I said, "I never want to sleep here,
If Robert is not on his side."

For more than sixty years,
The bed had been "our space"
With loving and holding, and closeness,
All our tomorrows it had helped us to face.

Then I looked on the floor near the window
Two pairs of bedroom shoes were there.
I picked them up and threw them away.
Never again will he need night shoes,
He is in the Land of Eternal Day.

I saw on the chest his eyeglasses,
For many years, he had need.
But now he has perfect knowledge,
He will no longer have to read.

Then I spied a little case with a charger,
His hearing aids were neatly inside.
No longer will he have trouble hearing,
For Jesus speaks close to his side.

At the table, his chair will be empty,
It's no fun to eat alone.
But I hear him say, "I am still with you,
Soon, we will be together at Home."

His legs that were so weak and trembly
Will no longer let him fall to the floor.
But he stands, straight and tall, and is calling,
"I am waiting on Heaven's bright shore.

I loved my family so dearly,
I want us together again,
I am counting on each one to meet me,
And we will never be parted again."

January 8, 2024

BRINGING US THROUGH

Death is strange in the feeling it leaves,
One is to rejoice, the other makes us grieve.
When we see our loved ones suffer so,
We think it would be easy to let them go.

But when Death comes and takes them away,
We wish for release, we had never prayed.
We know they are better, completely healed.
We know that to God's wisdom, we have to yield.

We never are ready to give them up,
To drink of this bitter and woeful cup.
Tho' God's ways are wise, He knows what is best;
We will never be ready to take this test.

Then He asks, "Will you trust Me, in all that I do,
And believe even in this, I will bring you through?"

So, our broken hearts and loneliness
Know deep inside, He will do what is best.
When we see nothing here to cling on,
We can run to the shelter of God's loving arms.

January 24, 2024

February

The Lord is nigh unto them that are of a broken heart.

Psalm 34:18

MISSING ROBERT

I thought I hurt when Robert died,
But little did I know,
That as the days and weeks went by
The pain would only grow.

I miss him more each day,
My heart feels torn in two.
I never thought that losing him
Would ever be this blue.

I look for him in every room
I hear his voice speaking,
I sense his presence in the bed
And for his arms, I'm reaching.

I know his days on earth are gone,
I know he won't return.
I know he's better off, by far;
But for him, my heart yearns.

If I could bring him back to me,
It would be a selfish thing;
He is happy, free, well, and whole.
Listening to the Angels sing.

February 6, 2024

MEMORIES

No matter what the Street Sign says,
no matter what its name; as I am driving in my car
alone, they all are "Memory Lane."
Every time I see a place, where we used to go to eat,
I think of all the fun times,
and it is a memory sweet.

I pass a yard where children play, my mind goes back a
long, long way, when our two played,
and ran the yard on every sunny day.

If I pass a Wedding Chapel, and the wedding party is
outside, my mind goes back to years ago
when I became a Bride.

At the Grocery Store, where I now shop alone;
I see him waiting in his chair,
To see what I'd bring home.
I see him getting frail, his heart is weak;
His strength is gone, his legs begin to fail.
I see his body growing thin, he cannot walk alone.
I put my arms around him, to help him move along.

But Jesus saw he needed help,
He said, "His time has come. I think he's suffered
long enough, so I will bring him home."
So, though I miss him being here
My heart is broken; my eyes have tears.
But I console myself in knowing
I will soon be where he is.

February 28, 2024

March

For whatsoever things that were written aforetime,
were written for our learning,
that we through patience, and comfort of the
Scriptures might have hope.

Romans 15:4

OUR ANNIVERSARY

Today is our Anniversary
We would celebrate year sixty-three;
A day I will cherish forever,
For you gave your heart to me.

We took our vows sincerely
For we knew our hearts were one;
Seems like just a short time ago,
Our journey had just begun.

The years went by so swiftly
Our family was raised and gone;
And we had so much time together—
We loved our time alone.

Then, aging and sickness overtook us,
The days passed by more swift
But our love grew deeper and stronger
For our hearts together were knit.

Then came the day I had dreaded
God took you to Heaven above.
I look forward to our next celebration
When there is peace, and eternal love.

March 4, 2024

Robert and Judy on their wedding day, March 4, 1961.

MISSING YOU

It's been nine weeks since you went Home,
And more than ever, I feel alone.
As days go by, my heart breaks more,
I wonder what the future has in store.

When in a crowd, I feel alone,
All I want is you, and home.
My arms ache to hold you tight,
My pillow's wet with tears at night.

I miss your smile, I miss your kiss;
I never knew how much I'd miss.
I always felt so loved and safe,
No one on earth could take your place.

I thank you for the years we had
The good times far outweighed the bad
I'm glad from pain you've been set free,
But how I miss you here with me.

I feel there's a hole when I once had a heart
Nothing is right when we are apart.
I know one day I will see your face,
So, I'll survive by God's Love, and Grace.

March 6, 2024

ALL ALONE

No matter how brightly the sun shines,
No matter if the sky is blue
No matter how crowded the room,
You feel it is only you.

When the one you loved so dearly
Has gone from your side, and your life;
Everything seems worthless and empty,
If you are missing the love of your life.

The lifetime of loving and sharing,
Together, you have always been.
And now, all that is left is heartbreak,
And longing to see them again.

The world is only temporal
Nothing lasts or stays the same,
You would give all that you own,
Just to hear your love call your name.

We cling to the hope of Heaven
Where parting will never come.
Our loved one is waiting to greet us,
And we will be forever at Home.

March 13, 2024

MISSING CHRISTMAS

It was almost Christmas, December twenty-third;
No tree lights were shining, no carols were heard.
No joy was found; it seemed nothing but gloom.
For my Love was dying in a hospital room.

It seemed so final, so helpless I felt,
He was fading before me, like a snowman melts.
I knew it was time; he had suffered so much,
But it was breaking my heart to lose his tender touch.

We had many years, his love was so true,
I could not imagine it was finally through.
The years had gone quickly, I could not give him up,
No one should drink from this bitter cup.

On New Year's Eve, he drew his last breath,
His life was over, his eyes closed in death.
It was such a sad day,
But his New Year began in a Glorious way.

No more suffering and pain,
No more trouble and strife.
He is happy and whole,
He has Eternal Life.

March 18, 2024

WHAT I MISS

I don't miss the things money can buy,
I miss the twinkle in his eye.
I don't miss seeing the sights,
I miss his arms, holding me tight.

I don't miss the places we went,
I miss the times together we spent.
I don't miss our travels and trips,
I miss the kisses from his sweet lips.

Things don't matter, nor what you own,
What you miss most, when your loved one is gone,
Is the love you shared, and the memories made.
They can never be taken by Death, or the Grave.

For in your heart, the memories live,
To make them alive, oh, what you would give.
But you can't live in sorrow and sadness and grief;
Just hold to the promise, that one day you will meet.

March 20, 2024

A VISIT

If I could be granted a wish
To have Robert for a brief time again,
But I had to choose the time frame,
For his visit on earth to begin…

Would I choose the days we first married,
When we were young and carefree,
Or the days when we were so busy,
With work, and a young family?

Or later in middle-age,
When once again we were free,
For the children were on their own now,
And we could do as we pleased?

Would I wish him back in old age,
With problems, and ills, and yet,
We spent all our time together,
Enjoying the days we had left?

Then stark reality hit me,
How selfish it would be,
To have him leave Heaven's splendor,
For just a moment with me!

Oh, no, I could never ask it,
Too much for him I care.
I will just have to wait to see him
Then, the Glories of Heaven, we'll share.

March 21, 2024

I WONDER

I know you are happy in Heaven,
I know from pain you are free,
But do you know how I miss you?
I wonder if my tears, you see.

I know there's no sorrow in Heaven
I know all is Joy complete,
But I wonder, do you think of the day,
When, once again, we will meet?

The Scripture tells us,
No sorrow in Heaven is known,
But will our life here be remembered,
Will we still to each other belong?

There, on a much higher plane
We will be,
But I wonder when we meet in Heaven,
Will your heart still belong to me?

March 25, 2024

MY EMPTY HEART

It is raining outside, the sky is gray
Like my heart has been since you went away.
Even when it is warm, and the sun shines bright
My heart is as dark as a moonless night.
You were my sunshine, you made the clouds go away,
You made the nighttime as bright as the day.

When we spent our days, always together,
It didn't matter the state of the weather.
No matter how dark the clouds in the skies,
The warmth of love was in your eyes.
I feel so alone, my heart is so bare,
Nothing counts if you are not there.
I try to be happy, keep a smile on my face,
But it's all just a front, without you in your place.

My arms want to hold you, your lips I want to kiss,
I never imagined how much I would miss.
We spent our lives always so close
To us, our love was what mattered the most.
I tried not to think of being alone,
For we were a pair, united as one.

Then came the time you had to leave,
Now I'm alone, and how my heart grieves.
Nothing is important, there's no real joy here;
I spend all my time wanting you near.
I know you are safe in Heaven above
Experiencing the joy of God's Eternal Love.
As much as I miss you, I am glad you are safe.
I'm waiting for the time when we meet face to face.

March 26, 2024

THE KING'S TABLE
Song of Solomon 1:12

If the King sits at His table
No matter what the spread.
It could be a bountiful feast,
Or maybe just water and bread.

The food is not important
What matters the most,
The King of Kings in His Glory,
Has consented to be our host.

We are invited to His table,
He treats us as honored guests.
No matter the food on the table,
We know it will be the best.

Just think, the King of Glory consented
To come to our humble home
And partake of a meal with us,
So, we never feel we are alone.

So, if your home seems so empty,
If there is no one present to share,
Just invite the "KING" to your table,
For He promised He would be there.

March 27, 2024

88 DAYS

They say eight is the number of a new beginning;
Number eighty-eight must have a special meaning.
It has been eighty-eight days since you went away
And the grief is as bad as the very first day.

I don't see ever starting anew
There's no point in trying when I'm not with you.
Each day I get up, I feel more alone
The house where we lived doesn't seem like home.

You were my security, my reason to live,
Now that you are gone, I have nothing to give.
You were the reason I was happy in life,
No joy compared with being your wife.

Our love grew stronger as the years went by;
We were always together, just you and I.
Sixty-three years we were privileged to share,
The future looks dark now that you are not here.

The "two become one" was never so true
The "one" left alone is so lonely and blue.
I can't bring you back,
I am glad you are happy and whole,
But where my heart once held you,
There is only a hole.

March 28, 2024

April

Lord make me to know mine end,
and the measure of my days,
what it is that I may know
how frail I am.

Psalm 39:4

TIME

If I could turn Time's Clock back,
What time would I want it to be,
Would I want the years before marriage
When I was young and carefree?

Would I want our early life
When children played at our feet?
Or would I want the middle years
When life for us was so sweet?

Would I want the years of Retirement
When we had so much time alone?
Yet we filled our days with happiness
And soon, the years had flown.

No matter what time we were spending,
No matter what we had to do,
I cherished each day and each moment
That I was spending with you.

Our "Time" together was ending
Your days of suffering were done,
Time for you has no meaning'
Eternal Life has begun.

April 2, 2024

TOO SOON OVER

Today was like our life
It started out sunny and clear.
But now the clouds are gathering
And the evening's close is near.

We started out young and carefree
All that mattered was being alone
Then, daily living caught us
And soon, the years had flown.
The pace and vigor of young days
Soon turned to problems of health;
And we couldn't stop time's aging
Even if we had had wealth.

Time waits for no man or reason,
No health is promised to stay.
It seems like the weeks pass so quickly
A year is like a few days.
We had many years together
And I tried not to think of the end;
But I knew when your heart started failing
We had not much time to spend.

If I could have kept you from leaving
It would have been so unfair;
For you were so tired and weary
With burdens of sickness to bear.
I am glad you are not suffering
I am glad you are happy and free.
But I'd give all that I own, and then some,
In your arms once more to be.

April 2, 2024

ALONE

I went to the doctor today
Where I took you so many times
It was a lonesome feeling
As the stairs to the office, I climbed.

The nurse greeted me so warmly
She gave me a sweet embrace
She was so sorry you had left us,
For no one could take your place.

I am glad you don't need the doctor,
I am glad you are completely healed.
But the fact that you are not with me
I find it hard to accept as real.

No matter where I go, or what I see
It doesn't feel right with you not with me.
We were always together, I was never alone;
If we were out, or just being at home.

I miss you so badly, my heart is so grieved;
But I know in God's mercy, He allowed you to leave.
You deserve to be free from life's toil and strife.
I am left with sweet memories of sharing your life.

April 4, 2024

ONE HUNDRED DAYS

One hundred years is a Century
Seems like a long, long, time
But one hundred days without you
Seems centuries to my heart and mind.

One hundred days since you left me
But you did not go alone,
For God sent the Angels to bring you
To Himself, and your Heavenly home.

It is so hard not to have you with me
My days and nights are so long.
But I know you are safe and happy
Being one of the Heavenly throng.

I can't wish you here to suffer
I am glad your spirit is free,
But oh, how I long to see you;
I miss you so here with me.

You ran your race with such patience
You continued to keep your sweet smile.
I am glad your suffering is over.
I will join you in just a while.

April 9, 2024

HEARTACHE

I think each day when I awaken
The loneliness won't be as bad
But the empty and lonely feeling
Each day is the worst I have had.

Each day I spend without you
Seems harder to get through
I long so much to see you
My heart is so sad, and so blue.

We had so much time together
But it never could be enough
My arms are aching to hold you.
Your lips, mine want to touch.

The house is so empty without you
The silence is so hard to bear.
This house will never be home
Without your presence to share.

So, I face each day with heartache;
My nights are long with little sleep.
I know you are waiting in Heaven
And I long for the day we will meet.

April 15, 2024

YOUR CLOTHES

I thought I could go through your clothes today
But when I took them out of the drawer,
I could not see for the tears that flowed
Remembering the times when you wore.

I know I can't keep them;
I know it would be unfair.
For there may be someone
Who has need of clothes to wear.

You don't need the clothes;
You are clad in garments of white.
You are basking in Heavenly Son-light
In the Land where there is no night.

So just as you shed this body of clay,
These clothes you have cast aside.
I can see you now in the garments of white.
You are part of Christ's Heavenly Bride.

April 18, 2024

NO LONGER A HOME

A house wasn't made for one alone
It takes at least two to make it a home.
It takes loving and living, and sharing the day,
Otherwise, a house is just a place to stay.

We had a home for a lot of years,
It was never lonesome, for you were here.
Now, it's nothing but silence and empty rooms
Filled with quietness, sadness, and gloom.

Silence seems to scream, "You are all alone."
Now, it's just a house; it is no longer a home.

You had no choice, it was time to go;
Your health was gone, and you suffered so.
I am glad you're no longer so tired and ill,
But I hate this empty house
Since your voice is stilled.

I sense your presence, I see your face,
My heart is longing for your warm embrace.

But God in His Mercy, allowed you to leave.
And He has promised comfort
For my heart that's so grieved.

April 20, 2024

LONESOME

I thought I knew what lonesome was,
I thought it meant being alone.
But lonesome is more than one being away,
It is a feeling you've never known.

If I go out for a visit or task
When I come back, there is no one to ask,
"How was your visit," or "What did you do?"
There's no one waiting who cares what you do.

An empty house is like a tomb
You feel you are buried in shadows of gloom.
The walls are silent, there is no one to speak,
It is always the same, week after week.

You were always waiting if I went out alone,
Always so happy to see me come home.
Now, I hate the silence and the empty space;
I'd give all that I own, just to see your face.

You can't return; so much happier you are,
The glories of Heaven are better by far.
You didn't leave of your own accord,
You heard the call from our wonderful Lord.

He said, "You have suffered enough; it is time for rest."
I know in my heart that God always knows best.
So, although I miss you, and I hate being alone.
I know you'll be waiting when I make it home.

April 28, 2024

May

For we know that if our earthly house
of this tabernacle were dissolved,
we have a building of God,
an house not made with hands,
eternal in the Heavens.

2 Corinthians 5:1

GOD KNOWS BEST

I miss you more today than I did yesterday,
I thought the pain would ease.
But each day you are away,
The more my heart still grieves.

I miss your voice, I miss your smile
I miss you being near.
Each day we are apart, I want you to be here.

I want your arms around me, I want your lips to kiss.
I want your presence in the room,
I never knew how much I'd miss.

I know you can't come back,
And would not if you could.
I know you are better off, by far
These facts are understood.

God was so merciful to take you Home
Your sickness is now healed.
I thank Him you are not in pain
To His wisdom, I must yield.

His ways are higher than our own
His Sovereignty will reign
So, I submit to what He does,
And soon, we'll meet again.

May 8, 2024

MOTHER'S DAY

My first Mother's Day without you
And the joy is not the same
You were always the first to greet me,
And thank me, again, and again.

You gave me two wonderful children
Who brought us so much joy.
A beautiful, precious daughter,
And a wonderful, loving boy.

You would be so very proud of them;
They so tenderly care for me.
You taught them to always be faithful
By example they could see.

So, I will spend the day with our children,
But oh, how you, we will miss.
I thank you for all that you gave us.
But I long for my Mother's Day kiss.

May 12, 2024

YOUR BIRTHDAY

Today, we would say, "Happy Birthday."
You would be ninety years old!
But you are celebrating in Heaven
In the Land where you will never grow old.

God gave us a long time together
Sixty-two of your birthdays we shared.
I tried each year to show you
How deeply for you I cared.

Now your birthdays on earth are over,
No longer will you age more each year.
For where you are now residing
The clock no longer appears.

Time is no more, just Eternal Life,
No more sickness, nor aging,
No sorrow, no strife.

But I will remember your birthday
And the beautiful memories we made,
They will stay in my heart forever
Till I see you some wonderful day.

I look forward to Heaven
For I know you are there;
And we will celebrate forever together
Where Eternal Life, we will share.

May 14, 2024

THE CLOSET

Today I cleaned out the closet
The racks were empty and bare
Now you are clothed in Heavenly garments,
No longer Earth's clothes you will wear.

Each garment I took from the hanger
Was a memory of you being here.
It was hard to give them away;
It was hard to hold back the tears.

I know you won't ever need them,
But it's a reminder that you are gone.
I wonder what you are wearing
As you worship around the Throne.

As I folded your shirts for the needy,
I could feel your arms in each sleeve.
I want you so much here with me
But I know you were ready to leave.

If your clothes can help the needy
Then I know what you would say,
"Give them all, I surely don't need them!
In robes of white, I'm arrayed."

May 18, 2024

A GIVING HEART

I took your clothes to the Thrift Store;
They can sell them to help the kids.
I knew you would want to help them,
For that is the way you lived.

When someone you heard had a need,
Your first desire was to help.
You were generous when it came to others,
But you never wanted things for yourself.

You lived your life so quietly
You never put on a show
If your children or I had a need
We knew to you we could go.

God loves a cheerful giver
And even in death, you still give.
A pattern you left, we can follow
Of the way our lives, we should live.

May 22, 2024

MEMORIAL DAY

Today is a Day of Remembrance
To those fallen in War.
But every day is a Day of Remembrance
Of the ones we lost, we adored.

Every day, I remember the wonderful life we had
It was not always a bed of roses,
But the good days far outweighed the bad.

I have so many memories
Of your loving and giving heart.
And each day I spend without you,
The more I hate we are apart.

The house is so empty without you
I see you in every space.
I miss your arms around me,
I miss the smile on your face.

But I must look to the future
When I see you in Heaven so fair;
Until we meet in the beautiful City
I will remember the wonderful life we shared.

May 27, 2024

June

Then we which are alive and remain
shall be caught up together with them
to meet the Lord in the air,
and so shall we ever be with the Lord.

2 Thessalonians 4:13

HEARTBREAK

When the ambulance came for Robert
I knew it would be his last ride.
I wanted to scream, "Don't take him!"
I felt like I died inside.
I phoned our daughter to come get me
She said we went to the E.R.
I don't remember going there;
I don't remember the trip in the car.
She said we stayed in E.R. with him
While they did all the exams and tests.
My next realization, I was losing the one I loved best.

I remember the week in the room,
watching his life ebb away.
I wasn't ready to face it; I never wanted this day.
He died, like he lived, so peacefully;
it seemed he just drifted away.
Inside, my heart was crying,
"You can't leave me, please stay."

The One who called him was stronger;
Our life and death He controls,
No matter how tightly I held him,
I was helpless when it came to his soul.

God took his weak and worn body
And removed his Eternal soul.
He took it to be with Him,
Where he walks on streets of pure gold.
I feel like my heart went with him;
Nothing matters since he is gone.
I console myself in knowing,
He will greet me when I make it home.

June 3, 2024

TEARS

Today, I miss you so badly
I have wanted to cry all day.
I thought with the passage of time
The grief would start going away.

But each day, when I awaken
To an empty house so quiet;
I miss your smile and your voice,
And I think it will never be right.

Your place at the table is empty
In bed, you are not on your side.
I try to stay busy without you,
But my tears, I just can't hide.

I know you are happy in Heaven
I am glad God set your soul free.
I know in His Mercy, He took you,
But I sure miss you here with me.

Though I can't keep the tears from falling,
And I can't stop the pain in my heart;
I will wait for reunion in Heaven,
And we will never again have to part.

June 6, 2024

THE WEDDING RING

I still wear my wedding ring
That my love is gone doesn't mean a thing.
A ring is a symbol of undying love,
I believe he still loves me, from Heaven above.

The ring stands for more than being a wife,
It symbolized the love that we shared in life.
The ring is a circle that has no end;
I feel from Heaven, his love he still sends.

In Heaven, we will know as we are known
To a much higher plane, our love will grow.
Not husband and wife, as we know here,
But eternally together, Heaven, we will share.

I know he is waiting
So his ring I will wear.
Till we're reunited forever
Heaven's glories to share.

June 10, 2024

FATHER'S DAY 2024

Father's Day is Sunday,
And your chair at the table we will miss.
Our children always came to greet you,
To give you a card, and a kiss.

They loved you sincerely and deeply
For they knew for them, you cared.
For more than sixty years
A Father's Day dinner we shared.

Now you are with your Father in Heaven
So much greater your day will be.
From things temporal and earthly,
Your soul has been set free.

We miss you not just this Sunday,
But daily, our hearts are grieved.
You were a wonderful earthly Father,
You deserve from pain to be free.

We long for the day when we see you
And never again be apart,
But especially this Father's Day Sunday,
We will hold you close in our hearts.

June 13, 2024

I HATE THE SILENCE

Today, I got up early
I had several things to do,
I was to take cookies to church
And I was going shopping for shoes.

I took the cookies to church;
I bought two pairs of shoes.
Then, I came home to an empty house,
And I felt my heart break anew.

I hate the house that's so empty;
Your voice I long so to hear.
There was no one to greet me when I entered,
And I couldn't hold back the tears.

I thought the miss would lessen
I thought I'd get used to you gone;
But every day, the pain grows more deeply
Each day, I feel more alone.

Our time together went swiftly;
I didn't think of being apart.
But where there were feelings of joy,
There is only a hole in my heart.

I know this life is temporal,
I know God gave us many years;
But until we're reunited in Heaven,
All I see ahead is more tears.

June 15, 2024

FEELING SAD

I can't quit crying today
The pain in my heart is so great
I always knew I would miss you;
But I never knew how much my heart would break.

It's been almost six months since you left me;
You would think the pain would be less real.
But each day, when I awaken
It seems my heart just won't heal.

I long for the day when I see you,
There is no joy in staying here.
I feel I am only half a person
Nothing matters or seems to be real.

I know my crying won't change things;
I wish you could have stayed strong.
But I know God, in His Mercy, took you,
For you had suffered so long.

I can't wish you here to suffer,
I am glad you have been released.
But I long for the day when I see you
And my sorrow and tears will have ceased.

June 19, 2024

MY THOUGHTS

I try to keep my mind busy
To keep thoughts of you away;
But no matter what I am involved in,
You never are far away.

No matter what I am doing,
No matter where I go;
There is an empty feeling
That wants and misses you so.

You never are out of my thinking
No matter how busy I can be,
I can converse with others,
But it is your face before me, I see.

I don't think the missing will get better,
I don't think my heart will ever heal.
For nothing can replace your presence,
And nothing will ever seem real.

I know you will never return,
I know you are happy and free.
But I will never again be complete
Till your face, once again, I see.

June 21, 2024

WHEN?

When will the pain go away?
When will I have a happy day?
When will I sleep the night through?
When will I ever quit missing you?

Maybe the pain will not hurt so,
Maybe one day, happiness will show.
Maybe one night, I will be able to sleep,
Maybe my eyes won't have to weep.

But now, it seems, every day I awake,
I want you more; my heart still aches.
I think today won't be so blue
But every day brings memories of you.

Everything I see is a memory we shared,
Every time I remember how much you cared.
Your love was true; you gave so much,
What I would give, to feel your touch.

I miss your presence, I miss your voice;
God called you Home, you had no choice.
For many years, we had a good life;
I know I was blessed to be your wife.

We had a long time, but it seemed so brief;
I wasn't ready to experience such grief.
My heart feels empty, my life seems in vain;
I will never be complete until I see you again.

June 24, 2024

WITHOUT YOU

I still don't want to eat at the table;
your vacant chair is too sad. For over sixty years,
you were present as husband and dad.
Now, if I sit at the table, I can't stand the empty space;
I want you to be present, I want to see your face.

When you became so ill, our sleeping arrangements
changed too. We moved to a different bedroom
to make it easier for you.
The bed we shared for so long holds only memories of
love; I don't want to sleep there alone
now that you are in Heaven above.
I tried one day to lie there; I thought I would take a
short sleep. But when my head hit the pillow,
all I could do was weep.

The memories of all that we shared came rushing into
my heart. I don't think I will ever sleep there,
now that we are apart.
Our life and love were so special; other people don't
understand. They don't believe our closeness
as we did life, hand in hand.

I never wanted to be without you;
I never wanted time away. I always wanted you with
me, when it came to the close of the day.

You didn't leave me by choice, you wanted me by your
side. I loved you with everything in me,
and my world fell apart when you died.

June 28, 2024

July

❤

Many waters cannot quench love,
Nor can the flood drown it.

Song of Solomon 8:7

NOT THE END

Today, I just feel restless;
There is nothing I want to do.
Everything seems pointless
If I can't spend time with you.

I washed the windows this morning,
I went shopping for a little while;
Then, I came home to an empty house,
And I missed your welcoming smile.

I visited a friend yesterday;
She is in a Nursing Home.
It made me so grateful to God,
That I never had to leave you alone.

We stayed at home together,
You were only out a few days;
Till God took you to your home in Heaven,
And for that, I give Him praise.

We had many years together;
We had all that we needed and more.
I believe we will be reunited,
For you are waiting on Heaven's Shore.

I miss you so here with me,
I know this is not the end.
I am eagerly waiting the day
We meet face to face, again.

July 6, 2024

TODAY

Today, I have missed you so badly;
I have been lonesome for you all day.
Each day, I find more reasons to miss you,
Every day is worse since you went away.

I miss you early in the morning,
I miss you at noon time too.
I miss you most in the evening,
When darkness brings feelings so blue.

I don't think I will ever be happy
Tho I put a smile on my face;
But nothing will ever bring joy,
I hate all this empty space.

I thank God for the years He gave us,
I thank Him for the life we shared.
We knew how we loved each other
And how much for each other we cared.

I will never quit wanting to see you
And hold you in my arms once more.
But I have to yield to God's wisdom
Till I meet you on Heaven's bright shore.

July 9, 2024

AN EMPTY HEART

I feel so empty
I feel so blue,
I feel no purpose
In a life without you.

I spend time with friends,
I shop at the store;
But the lonely feeling
Is just there, even more.

I don't want things,
I don't want trips,
I want your arms
I want your kiss.

I want you here
Though I know it can't be;
I know you are healed,
I know you are free.

I wasn't ready for you to leave,
I can't stand how my heart grieves.
I know God rules, I know He cares;
But this empty heart is too much to bear.

July 10, 2024

GOD RULES

God doesn't ask what we want.
He does what He knows is best.
Sometimes, what we face
Would not be our request.

When He takes the light of our life,
A child, or a husband, or maybe a wife,
We think it's not fair; we would never agree.
But He knows what He is doing—
He doesn't ask you or me.

Life and Death are in His Mighty Hand
We have to submit, though we don't understand.
When the veil is removed
And all things are made clear,
Then, we will know the reason
For these heartaches and tears.

July 14, 2024

LOVING CARE

We never had a need you did not provide;
All my problems to you I could confide.
More than a husband, you were my best friend.
No matter what life dealt us,
On you, I could depend.

I was so blessed to be your wife,
For so many years to share your life.
On your steadfast love, I could always depend;
I never wanted it to end.

Now you are home with God
And I am alone
Now I live in just a house,
For you made it a home.

It will never be the same
Since you are not here.
My heart is so empty,
My eyes full of tears.

July 14, 2024

LIFE

We met when I was just a teen,
Though seven years more, he had seen.

We fell in love, though sometimes not;
I thought for him was best forgot

But soon, the truth came clearly out;
He was the One, there was no doubt.
.
I moved away far out of town;
But being persuaded, donned wedding gown.

The years went by, we both were old;
Our tale in life would soon be told.

He was the first to say goodbye,
Left me with broken heart and tear-filled eyes.

Now, I am left with memories sweet;
One day I know, again we'll meet.

July 17, 2024

OUR BED

Last night I did something
That for months made me dread.
I decided to go back to our room
And sleep again in our bed.

For more than sixty years
The bed had been our space;
No matter what the day had brought us
We were safe in our love and embrace.

The bed had a special meaning
For it was our time alone.
And our sleep was sweet and restful,
To each other, we knew we belonged.

When the time came for your leaving,
I knew you could no longer stay.
My heart and my love went with you
The day God took you away.

Now your side of the bed is empty,
No longer in your arms can I be.
Though I want you so here with me,
I am glad from sickness you are free.

I look forward to the day I see you
And we will be together again;
There will be no beds in Heaven
For Eternal Day has no end.

July 20, 2024

MISSING YOUR PRESENCE

I went to a dinner at church today
And my heart started hurting anew;
For the memories of all the times before
When I sat at the table with you.

Then I came home to our empty house,
And I hated the quietness and still.
I don't think I will ever be happy again—
Life without you is just not real.

Nothing means anything since you are gone;
I hate this feeling of being alone.
I want to see the smile on your face,
I want to feel your warm embrace.

I look at your pictures and see your smile,
Some are with family and friends.
We shared good times and enjoyed life,
I never wanted it to end.

Each day I awake, the sadness is here,
The empty feelings and falling tears.
I feel so alone, I want you so much;
Life seems useless without your loving touch.

July 21, 2024

THE SWING

When the day was ending, and chores were done,
Evening was falling and setting the sun,
In the backyard was an old porch swing
Where we spent time together, sometimes,
not saying a thing.

Just sitting quietly in the evening chill,
Watching the moon rise over the hill.
No need for words or idle chatter,
Being together was all that mattered.

We spent many evenings in that old swing;
Didn't need to be out, or shopping for things.
We had what we wanted, just us two alone,
Not realizing then, how the time had flown.

If we had a quarrel or disagreed,
This time alone was all we would need,
To remind us again how much we cared,
So precious this time, in the swing we shared.

Now the old swing is gone, and so is my love,
We will meet again in Heaven above.
In perfect love forever, we will be,
Enjoying God's goodness for all eternity.

July 30, 2024

SEVEN SAD MONTHS

Seven months ago today
God took you to be with Him.
Seven months ago today,
I walked through shadows dim.

The hardest day I ever spent
Was seven months ago;
I watched you leave; you could not stay—
I never felt such woe.

We walked life's path together
For more than sixty years;
You left for glorious sights to see
But I was left with tears.

I'd like to know what you are seeing;
I know 'tis wondrous to behold.
You are walking in the Heavenly Light
On streets paved with pure gold.

I cannot wish you back
Though my heart is torn in two.
You can't come back to me,
So soon, I'll come to you.

July 31, 2024

August

And I heard a voice from Heaven saying unto me,
Write, Blessed are the dead which die in the Lord,
from henceforth: Yea saith the Spirit,
that they may rest from their labors,
and their works do follow them.

Revelation 14:13

AUGUST

We are in the month of August;
It was the month we met.
It was Sunday, the sixteenth, a day I won't forget.

I liked you from the start; I knew it would be love.
I feel that you were sent to me
From our Heavenly Father above.

At first, it was not smooth sailing;
We had our ups and downs
And when I really knew I wanted you,
I had moved far out of town.

But as the days and weeks went by,
You realized you felt the same.
You asked me to return to you,
And wed and take your name.

So many years ago, it seems like yesterday.
The years passed by so quickly,
And you had to go away.

Now I am left without you
And the miss is hard to bear;
You are safe and happy in Heaven,
You've left behind all toil and cares.

But I know again I will see you,
The Scriptures have made it clear;
That we will know as we are known in Heaven
And I know you are waiting there.

August 6, 2024

WHY AUGUST IS SPECIAL

On a Sunday afternoon in August
My life was forever changed,
My friend introduced me to a guy;
Robert was his name.

I liked him from the start, though we did not always agree,
But soon, my heart convinced me He was the One for me.

Only seventeen months later, I became his bride,
For more than sixty years, He was faithful by my side.

For almost sixty-three years
I was blessed to share his life
I give thanks to God each day
That he chose me for his wife.

With two children, we were blessed,
Then, grandchildren numbered four
And soon, five great-grandchildren blessed us even more.

We had sickness and daily problems that life brings to all
But each time there was a need, God saw us through it all.

Then came the time of sorrow,
When parting days drew near;
His health began to fail
And I knew he could not stay here.

It tore my heart apart
To see him leave my side.
But I give thanks to God above
For the day I became his bride.

August 14, 2024

A DAY TO REMEMBER

Sixty-five years ago today I met the love of my life;
Seventeen months later, I became his wife.

The years went by so swiftly
And when our time together would end,
I was not ready to let him go
I needed him and loved him so.

We had our days of not-so-sweet,
But no matter what, our hearts would meet.
For we knew together, we belonged
We always fixed the feelings of wrong.

If we disagreed, we worked it out,
For we knew we loved, without a doubt.
A kiss, a hug, a word from the heart
Quickly fixed our feelings apart.

When old age came, our love grew deeper,
Our fellowship was even sweeter.
We truly had become as one
I wasn't ready to see it "done."

The day he left, it broke my heart;
I never wanted us apart.
He had become so ill and weak
So he answered the call when he heard God speak.

God said, "You lived your life so true
And now there's rest, and peace for you."
So he left to be with God above
But he will always be my one true love.

August 16, 2024

JUST WHEN

Just when I think my heart will heal
The absence of you becomes more real.
Just when I think I won't cry today,
Something reminds me that you are away.

Just when I think that life will go on,
That in my heart, there may be a song,
Then something reminds me so much of you,
And the sunshine is gone, and life is still blue.

Just when I think, tonight I can sleep,
When my head hits the pillow, I start to weep.
I feel your presence in the bed we shared
I remember your love, and how much we cared.

Just when I think of chores to do
I remember, no need to hurry back to you.
You are no longer waiting for me to return
I miss you so; for you, my heart yearns

Life has no joy since you went away;
Nothing but loneliness, day after day.
I wonder if my heart will ever heal,
For now, nothing is right, and nothing is real.

August 21, 2024

Robert picking up apples with his grandson, Andrew.
(June 2002)

THE JUNE APPLE TREE

He planted the apple tree many years ago,
Sat back a few years and watched it grow.
Then, one year, the tree started to bear
Beautiful June apples, so many were there.

Sweet red applesauce we froze each year,
The grandkids loved it when they were here.
We gave many apples to friends around
For the June apples covered much of the ground.

The years went by, and the tree grew old
Like the one who planted it so long ago.
In later years, just a few apples grew;
The tree, like the Planter, was nearly through.

In the past few years, only a few apples were found;
The tree's limbs died, and all turned brown,
No longer apples on it were found.
It had served its purpose for a lot of years,
Now, the end of the tree was drawing near.

Seems like the tree somehow knows
The man who planted it so long ago
No longer needs the fruit it bore.
Now he has fruit from the Tree of Life evermore.

August 26, 2024

ANOTHER DAY ALONE

I miss Robert more today
Than anytime since he went away.
I look at his pictures and his smiling face;
I long so much to feel his embrace.

I want him here to hear his voice;
I know he didn't leave by choice.
I can't stand us being apart;
I want him in my arms, not just in my heart.

It seems so long he's been away,
I miss him more each passing day.
I always knew one day this would be,
I'd give all I own if his face I could see.

Nothing is important or matters to me
If in his arms, I will never be.
He was my life, my reason to be;
I know without him, there's no joy for me.

August 28, 2024

September

I will not leave you comfortless:
I will come to you.

John 14:18

SOMEDAY

Someday, I think my heart will heal,
That I will accept what I know is real.
But my heart has a mind of its own,
And it will never accept the fact you are gone.

I walk in the house after being out
And the silence is deafening, it seems to shout,
"You are all alone; your love is not here."
My heart breaks anew, and my eyes fill with tears.

They say time will heal all our sorrows,
That someday will be a brighter tomorrow
That one day, I will accept my life without you,
But so far, this fact, to me, is not true.

We had many years, our love was so true;
When you saw one, you always saw two.
We never wanted to be apart;
Now, I am left alone
With an empty, broken heart.

September 1, 2024

SEPTEMBER

Today, the calendar says September first;
Starting nine months since you left this earth.
It seems like a century since I saw your face
Or heard your voice or felt your embrace.

Each day, I awaken to a house so still
The fact you aren't here is still not real.
My life has no purpose, no joy I find;
The memory of you never leaves my mind.

Wherever I go, whatever I do
Has no meaning if I can't have you.

I know you are happy;
From sickness, you are healed
I know God in His Goodness
has made Heaven real.

I don't wish you back to this world of woe;
But as long as I live
I will still miss you so.

September 1, 2024

HIS LIFE

When I had a hard day, and things had gone wrong,
He'd take me in his loving arms,
Tell me everything would be okay;
Kiss all my tears and worries away.

Trinkets and gifts he seldom would buy,
But we never had a need, he did not supply.
He loved me and the children so much;
Gave what we needed—his tender touch.

He wasn't a gabber, his tongue was not glib;
But his life, not his words, proved how he lived.
So many memories, so many years,
To live them again,
Oh, what I would give.

September 3, 2024

LOOKING BACK

Today, I am grateful
That from sickness you are free.
I am glad you no longer suffer;
But I still want you here with me.

We had many years to enjoy
Before old age and sickness arrived.
We never had real problems or worries,
Life's ups and downs, we survived.

I am glad God joined us together
And the bond, we never wanted to break.
I knew when we fell in love
I had found my life's soul mate.

I thank you for all that you gave me
Your love was so faithful and true
If I could go back through the years,
I would still spend my life with you.

Now you've left me here without you,
Though it wasn't your choice to make.
I will never be happy without you,
For your presence and love, my heart aches

September 6, 2024

DOES JESUS CARE

We sing the song, "Does Jesus Care?"
When we've said goodbye to the one we loved best.
Does He share our grief? Does His heart break?
In His arms, can we really rest?

We know He cares, His heart is grieved;
His promises assure us He will never leave.
When we feel so alone, and empty inside
We find it hard to believe.

We think no one could feel how much we hurt,
Though we know that is why He came to earth;
To feel our pain and our sorrow share,
He truly knows; He has been there.

So, when we feel we are all alone,
He is praying for us on His heavenly throne.
He promised never to leave our side,
In His comforting love, He allows us to hide.

He promised in sorrow to see us through;
He said, "I will not leave you comfortless,
I will come to you."
Like the robin who covers her young in the nest
We are under His wings and can lean on His breast.

September 13, 2024

DREAMS

Many nights, I dream about you
And wish that I could stay asleep;
Because when I awaken,
You won't be here, for me to keep.

Doesn't matter what the dream's about,
Doesn't matter the dream's weather.
What matters in the dream,
We are still together.

But soon the dream is over
And I find I am alone;
I lie awake in darkness
Waiting for the dawn.

I think God lets me dream;
He lets me see your face.
He is assuring me
You are safe in His embrace.

One day, my dreams, in Heaven,
Will become reality.
When earthly nights are over,
We'll spend Eternity.

September 15, 2024

IF I KNEW

If I knew December twenty-second
Would be the last night together we would spend,
And if I knew in just a week
Your life on earth would end…

I would ask God to stay the darkness,
Ask Him to hold back the dawn,
If I knew when morning came
You would forever leave our home.

If I knew again, I would never hold you
Or plant a kiss upon your cheek,
Though I knew your heart was failing
And you were so tired and weak…

I would ask God to wait a day
Or two or three or four,
A short reprieve, a time to grieve
Before you left through our front door.

I am glad God doesn't tell us
In His wisdom, He cares too much
To give to us the knowledge
When we will lose our loved one's touch.

I know it was His mercy
That allowed you to leave life's pain;
I thank Him for the promise
That I will see you soon, again.

September 19, 2024

LETTING GO

Last night, I cried myself to sleep
This morning, I woke with more tears.
Each day, I find I miss you more
You'll soon be gone a year.

The days and nights are so long
I try to stay busy, and yet,
You never leave my heart and mind,
Your smile I cannot forget.

You were so sick and helpless;
I know your days were long.
But you never gave up, or quit trying,
For me, you tried to stay strong.

It was hard to watch you suffer,
But harder to let you go.
I know it was selfish to want you to stay;
But I wanted and needed you so.

But God had a plan, and He knows best,
He knew your days were through;
So, in mercy and love, He set you free;
But my heart still yearns for you.

September 19, 2024

THE SEASONS

You always loved the Springtime,
You like to see things grow.
You didn't like the Winter
When the cold north winds would blow.

You couldn't wait for Springtime
And your garden you could till;
So many veggies you would grow.
So many jars we'd fill.

You dreaded to see Fall come,
Though you loved its beauty rare
But you knew cold days were coming,
And for them, you didn't care.

Now the leaves are falling;
Soon, Winter will be here.
But where you are is Springtime
There's no Seasons changing there.

No days, no nights, no changing,
Eternal light and bliss.
No leaves to rake, or gardens sow,
No Wintertime to miss.

The sun won't have to shine,
The moon won't have to glow;
Only Heavenly rays of gladness,
Where Eternal flowers grow.

September 20, 2024

THE END OF THE TREE

They are coming today
To cut down the June Apple tree.
I am glad you won't have to see.
You loved that tree you put in the ground
It will be sad to know it is no longer around.

For trees, like people, fade away
For nothing on earth is here to stay.
The tree served you well for many years;
Now, the tree, like you, will no longer be here.

The Tree of Life has twelve manner of fruit
Everyone's taste buds, it will suit.
I think when you eat from the Tree of Life,
It will taste like June Apples
For that's what you liked.

When the saw starts taking down the tree,
I don't want to watch, I don't want to see.
I can see you gathering apples from the ground,
Its absence is a sad reminder
That you aren't around.

September 23, 2024

RAINY DAYS

Rainy days were special days
For we could be alone.
Too wet to work, nowhere to go,
We were together at home.

Our time alone, a time to love;
We loved the days inside.
Just being together, just us two,
All alone, till the rain was through.

Now, rainy days are dreary and sad
Remembering the past, and the days we had.
Now I am alone
with thoughts of you
Rainy days now, only make me blue.

I miss our days, I miss our times,
I don't like being alone.
Sunshine or rain, it doesn't matter
If I can't have you at home.

All I have are memories sweet
Of the life and love we had.
I long for the time I see you again.
And I will never again be sad.

September 24, 2024

STORMS

When a bad storm was coming, I still felt safe.
I knew you were here, I was in your embrace.
But now, when the lightning flashes
and the thunder roars
Your arms aren't here, to make me feel secure.

The thunderstorms and problems of life
Never scared me, for I was your wife.
Now, I am alone to face my fears;
You are gone, but I know God is still here.

It was God who kept us both safe from fear
No matter the storms, we knew He was near.
God was always in charge of all that we faced
No matter the storms, we were safe in His embrace.

It's a different feeling now to face storms alone;
You were always here, I felt no alarm.

I am glad you are safe,
From life's storms, you are free.
But when the lightning flashcs
I miss you here with me.

But God, who kept us both in His care,
Has promised in storms, He will always be there.
So, I will pillow my head and try to sleep
For my fears and my worries,
He has promised to keep.

September 25, 2024

MY FEARS

I am alone in the storm
The neighbors are gracious to help
But with you not here, I feel alone;
I feel I am by myself.

But you were weak,
You were suffering so;
I am glad you are delivered.
Through this, I am glad you won't go.

I miss your presence,
You made me feel safe;
You always calmed my fears.
I wasn't afraid, no matter what came
As long as you were near.

But I am not alone
For there is One who never leaves;
God promised His presence,
His help, and His love, to all who believe.

I know He is in charge
Of whatever we face ahead,
So, I'll trust His Mercy,
His Grace, and His Love,
For He always does what He said.

September 30, 2024

THIS TOO WILL PASS

Three days ago, the sky was dark,
the winds were fierce.
It was raining in sheets, the trees were falling,
The flood waters came.
The earth's terrain forever was changed.

Houses swept away,
Bridges snapped, and roads washed away,
Many were evacuated
In their homes, not able to stay.

Today, the sun is shining
The sky is a beautiful blue;
The winds are calm, the rains are gone,
The storm has passed on through.

It is like our lives as we go through storms
Of sickness, and sorrow, and grief;
It won't be long till "The Son" appears
Bringing eternal glory and relief.

The storm left its mark,
Many needs still not met,
But when "The Son" shines,
There will be no needs,
No sorrow, no grief, no regrets.

September 30, 2024

October

Why art thou cast down O my soul?
And why art thou disquieted within me?
Hope thou in God, for I shall yet praise Him,
who is the health of my countenance,
and my God.

Psalm 42:11

WAITING FOR TOMORROW

Today, I wish you were with me;
I am visiting David and Joan.
I am staying a few days with them,
There's no power or water at home.

It is strange to be here without you;
You loved to come to see them
Though our visits were far too few.

My life still seems so empty;
I miss you being with me.
I love being with our family,
But it's your face I want to see.

I know you would say, "Go see them,
Have a good time, have fun!"
But for me, life has no real joy
Since God has taken you home.

I know you are happy
You ran your race so true
I am glad you no longer suffer
But life is not real without you.

I don't wish you back to Earth's sorrow;
I am glad God set your soul free.
So, I'll wait for the glad tomorrow
When together, forever, we'll be.

October 7, 2024

HAPPINESS AND JOY

Happiness and joy are not the same.
Happiness is temporary, Joy does not change.

Happiness depends on
What happens throughout the day;
Joy is a gift from God
That never goes away.

Happiness is an emotion
When life is going our way.
Joy is our strength to help
In whatever comes our way.

We are not always happy;
Circumstances change the way we feel.
But Joy is within our hearts,
Our assurance God is real.

We all have grief,
We all have sorrow.
But with joy, there is no fear
Of what may come tomorrow.

Happiness is good, we all need fun;
It helps relieve life's stress.
But with never-ending joy
We know our God will bless.

October 9, 2024

COMING HOME

I had to leave our home to get out of the storm;
I was gone for nine days.
The kids didn't want me alone
So, David took me away.

I stayed almost a week with David
Then, at Sheila's, a few days more
But it felt good to come to our home,
I knew when I opened the door.

But a feeling of sadness engulfed me,
For again, I felt so alone;
I missed you being with me,
I need you to make it our home.

But I know where you are is better,
I know you are happy and free.
I thank you for the home you gave me,
I just wish your face I could see.

I will never be happy without you;
I will never be complete, or whole.
But I know one day I'll be with you
While the years of Eternity roll.

October 10, 2024

NEVER ENOUGH TIME

I want to cry this evening;
I am so sad and blue.
I went away for awhile
And came home and missed you anew.

If we went away, it was together;
And we looked forward to coming home.
But when I returned by myself,
I never felt so alone.

I know you will never be here,
I know I will face life alone;
I know I will have to be patient
Till I see you when I make it home.

I am glad you no longer suffer;
I just wish you could have stayed strong.
But I have to thank God for His blessings,
For the life He gave us, was long.

No matter how much time He gave us
I would always have wanted more;
But I cling to the hope of the promise
You are waiting on Heaven's shore.

October 10, 2024

WAITING

The year is nearly over
Only seventy-nine days remain,
Until it will be a year ago
God called you home, by name.

Nearly a year ago, you left me,
And it hurts just as bad today;
My heart broke in a thousand pieces
The day you went away.

I thought time would ease the sorrow,
I thought the pain would not hurt so.
But every day the sun rises,
I still don't want you to go.

I know you are in God's presence,
I am happy you are well, and free;
I know it was God's love and mercy
That He set your spirit free.

I long for the time when I see you
And we won't have to part anymore;
I feel you are waiting for me
To join you on Heaven's bright shore.

October 13, 2024

THE TOUCH OF YOUR HAND

I still can't get used to the silence;
It deafens me when I come home.
It only adds to the reality
That I really am all alone.

I eat my meals in silence;
There is no one to laugh or talk.
This path of being lonely
Is one I never wanted to walk.

I just pictured us always together;
I thought our life together we would spend.
But I know what they say is true,
"Good things always come to an end."

Now you've gone ahead without me,
For that is what God had planned.
But it sure is lonely without you;
I need the touch of your hand.

October 13, 2024

OUR HOME

I came home from church today,
And the house was silent and still.
I am still not used to you being gone;
I don't think I ever will.

For nearly sixty years
This was the home we shared,
It is a welcoming, pleasant home,
For you made it with much care.

In every room of the house
I see the work of your hands;
You did so much through the years—
Hard work, you did understand.

It isn't large or fancy
But it is furnished with love and care;
What endears this home to me,
Is that it's the home we shared.

Now your new home is a mansion
That God has provided with love.
I will cherish the home that you gave me
Till we share our new home above.

October 13, 2024

FALL

The Fall of the year is upon us;
The trees have hardly a leaf.
It is hard to believe summer is gone,
Summertime seemed so brief.

We know winter will surely follow,
The days much shorter will be;
The Seasons change so quickly,
Like the lives of you and me.

The Springtime of youth is happy,
The sunshiny days are long;
We have no cares or troubles,
Our hearts are filled with song.

But when the Seasons start changing,
Each Season seems more brief,
Soon wintertime is upon us,
And we face life's sorrows and griefs.

Our lives are like a vapor,
They rise and soon fade away.
Old age, we begin to experience,
Soon, we will come to the end of our days.

But when we leave Earth's Seasons,
We will go where time is no more.
For days and nights aren't measured,
Just Eternal Life, evermore.

October 16, 2024

I WONDER

Today, I have been so lonely;
All day, I have wanted to cry.
I know you are happy in Heaven
Above the October blue sky.

I look at the clouds and wonder,
Back to earth, are you permitted to see?
Do you have any thoughts or knowledge
Of what is going on with me?

I know old things are passed,
I know everything is made new,
But I wonder, are you aware
Of how my heart aches for you?

I wonder about the future,
I know we will know as we're known;
But will we enjoy Heaven together
Will we share a Heavenly home?

I know all things earthly are over,
I know from everything here we'll be free;
But when I see you in Heaven
Will your heart still belong to me?

October 19, 2024

STILL MISSING YOU

Today, I tried to stay busy,
I tried not to think about you.
But your face was always before me
No matter what I tried to do.

I ate breakfast alone at the table,
I could see you there in your chair.
My lunch I ate on the sofa,
But I could see your tray and your chair.

I made the bed this morning,
Your side was not even turned down;
I hate the emptiness and silence,
I still want you around.

Now it's getting late in the evening,
It will soon be time for bed.
And the quietness and darkness will be here;
The nights are what I most dread.

It will soon be a year since you left me,
And the miss is harder each day.
I never wanted to be apart from you,
Life is no fun since you are away.

I know in this life I won't see you,
I know you cannot return;
I wonder if you know how I miss you
How much for you, my heart yearns.

October 23, 2024

TEN MONTHS

Ten months ago today you left here,
The ambulance took you away.
It was the day my heart died within me,
For I knew it was our last day.

Your last day at home with me
I never have felt such pain;
I knew when the ambulance left here
You would never be home again.

I still can't stop the tears from falling,
My heart is so empty and bare.
I know God, in His Mercy, took you,
For you needed more than my care.

I thank Him for all that He gave us,
Your life and our marriage were long
But my heart is so broken and sad,
I don't think it will ever have a song.

I guess I loved you too deeply;
Our lives were so intertwined.
My arms are so empty without you,
You're forever in my heart and my mind.

October 23, 2024

REUNION

It seems so long since you left me,
So long we have been apart;
The more days I spend without you,
The greater the pain in my heart.

On the walls, I see your pictures;
They make me wish you were here.
They bring memories of sweet times together
When I thought you would always be near.

I wasn't ready to lose you
But God had a different plan;
He knew too long you had suffered,
Now you are safe in His mighty Hand.

I am glad your sickness is over,
I am glad from pain you're released.
You are happy and whole in Heaven,
Your sufferings and trials have ceased.

I can't wish you back to Earth's sorrow
Tho I miss you so here with me;
I will wait till I meet you in Heaven,
What a glad reunion it will be.

October 25, 2024

ANOTHER WEEK

It is Saturday night again,
Another week is gone
Seven lonely days have passed,
That I hated being alone.

October is almost over,
Soon, you will be gone for a year.
The hardest year I've ever spent;
I still can't believe you aren't here.

I try to fill my days,
Try to find something to do.
But nothing satisfies my heart,
All I want is you.

I know I am being selfish,
But I love and miss you so;
I always knew the time would come
I would have to let you go.

God was so merciful to set you free.
Your strength was gone; your days were through.
He said, "You have suffered long enough.
There is peace and rest for you."

So, He took you home to be with Him,
You deserve to be at rest.
I know He always does what is right
His way is always best.

October 26, 2024

November

And God shall wipe away all tears from their eyes,
and there shall be no more death, neither sorrow,
nor crying, neither shall there be any more pain,
for the former things are passed away.

Revelation 21:4

Today is the first day of November 2024.

I awakened with a different feeling in my heart. I thought of Robert the moment I woke up, as I have every day since he left this earth.

I live in what, in my mind, is the most beautiful part of the world God made. A few weeks ago, this beautiful land was ripped apart with torrential rains, tornados, and a hurricane named Helene. A lot of the countryside now is deep gullies, mud fields, treeless banks, houses and businesses that are destroyed and gone.

The land is like our heart feels when Death takes our loved ones: empty, barren, and desolate.

Just as people help others and clear away debris, God's Mercy and Grace somehow remove the ugliness of death from our hearts. Many homes will never be replaced, but others will be rebuilt more beautiful than they were.

There will never be a moment my heart will not long to be with Robert. There will never be a day I won't miss his presence. Just as the losses people suffered in the storm will never be replaced.

But they will survive.

I wrote in June that I never wanted to sleep again in the bed we shared for more than sixty years. Yet, by the end of July, I returned to our bed, and a feeling of closeness and peace, I found.

We can't run from our memories. We must wrap them around us as blankets of comfort. So, I am trying to let my memories, my longings, and the emptiness in my heart, be filled with anticipation of what lies ahead.

I have to look forward to seeing and being with Robert again in Heaven. The Bible says we will know as we are known. Heaven is far better than anything on Earth, so however our relationship in Heaven will be, it will exceed the joy and happiness we shared for nearly sixty-three years on earth. Although I will continue to grieve, and my heart will hurt, I will look forward to our reunion in Heaven.

REUNITED

There will never be a day I won't miss you,
Never be a day my heart won't hurt.
Never be a time, as long as I live,
I won't long for the life we shared on earth.

I know my grief is selfish,
For it's all about my tears and my sorrows;
I will try to live in anticipation
Of what is waiting in God's tomorrow.

We had many years together,
Our love was constant and true.
So, I will look for the glad tomorrow,
When all grief and sorrow is through.

November 1, 2024

STILL SAD

I thought my heart was healing,
I thought the pain was less real;
But this morning, I can't quit crying,
Loneliness is all I can feel.

I try so hard to be happy,
I try to sing a glad song;
But every day I spend without you
The more everything seems wrong.

I do thank God you are happy,
I thank Him from sickness you are free.
But I feel I am only half a person
Since you are not here with me.

I went to the store to get busy,
I thought, "I won't cry if I am out."
But as soon as I had to return,
The tears fell when I entered the house.

I don't think I will ever be happy,
I don't think I will ever feel whole;
For I feel my heart went with you,
In its place is only a hole.

I said I was going to do better,
I said I will try to be glad.
But I long so much to be with you,
Today, I am still so sad.

November 4, 2024

EACH LONELY DAY

Each day that passes, I feel more alone;
I hate waking up knowing you are gone.
I hate the house so still and quiet;
It is bad all day, and worse at night.

I miss you more each day I live;
To see you again, oh, what I would give!
I wish I could change the clock of time,
And live again the days of our prime.

I don't wish you back to be sick and weak,
When you were so tired you could barely speak.
I want you back like years ago,
When life was fun, and we loved so.

But God knows best, He is in charge of life;
He gave me many years to be your wife.
So, I thank Him for all the blessings we shared,
I loved you so, and for me, you cared.

November 9, 2024

FORTY DAYS

This time last year, I had no idea
That in forty days, you would not be here.
I knew you were weak, and your days were few,
But I didn't know how soon I'd lose you.

Today, it still hurts so
Though, I know it was time for you to go.
I wasn't ready to be apart
When you left, you took with you
My broken heart.

I know I have to continue on,
No matter how I hate being alone.
I just have to give thanks for the years we had;
But my life without you is so very sad.

I remember the closeness of all we shared;
I know how deeply for each other we cared.
We were so blessed with many years;
Though the memories are sweet, I still have tears.

I don't cry for you, for you are at Home;
I cry for myself that you left alone.
But God was good to set you free;
I just long for the day when your face I see.

November 9, 2024

YOUR BEST CHRISTMAS

We are in the month of November;
Christmas will soon be here.
The year has passed so quickly,
Yet it seems like a hundred years.

This time last year, you were failing;
Your life was nearly through.
Now, it will be another Christmas
I have to spend without you.

Last year you were leaving at Christmas;
You had less than a week to live.
It was the worst Christmas of my lifetime;
To change it, oh, what I would give.
.
You spent the New Year in Heaven,
Though time is not measured there.
I cannot imagine the wonders
You've seen of beauties so rare.

This Christmas, my heart will be empty,
For you won't be here with me.
Your Christmas will be so wonderful,
With the Christ of Christmas, you'll be.

November 11, 2024

YOUR CHAIR

The last year of your life, you were so patient;
You sat in your chair all day.
It must have been so monotonous
Waiting for the hours to pass away.

You never complained or got angry,
You never lost the smile on your face.
The only way you could have survived it,
Was that you knew the touch of God's Grace.

You were almost completely helpless,
And I still can't understand;
How patiently you depended on others,
You never made a demand.

You were so gracious and thankful,
It was breaking my heart, for I knew;
Our time together was ending,
And your life would soon be through.

I know God kept you so sweet in your spirit
As you sat in your chair day by day.
So, one day, God said, "That's enough."
And He lovingly took you away.

You witnessed His Grace to others
By the smile you kept on your face
You showed your family and others
The strength of Mercy and Grace.

Now your chair is a reminder
That you are no longer here.
You showed everyone who knew you,
How to face Death, with no fear.

November 16, 2024

CHANGE

Today the weather is changing,
The skies are cloudy and gray;
Yesterday's sun is hidden from view,
Wintertime is on its way.

The warm days of summer have disappeared;
The wind is brisk and cold.
The leaves have fallen, the trees are bare;
The Summer's Tale is told.

It is like our lives, which change so fast,
We think the days of youth will stay,
We find so quickly our health is gone,
And our lives are passing away.

The people we love, and are joined in heart,
We think, "Together, we'll always be."
But life is brief, and too soon they leave,
We are left with a heart that grieves.

To have them stay would be our desire
Though we know this cannot be;
They leave behind all worries and cares,
Forever, they are free.

We feel deserted and left alone,
Though by choice, they did not go.
They answered the call when God bid them, "Come!"
Now they are waiting for us at Home.

But Springtime will come, and the sun will shine,
The flowers and leaves will appear.
So, we will trust, and leave it in the hands of God
And face wintertime with no fear.

November 21, 2024

THANKSGIVING

Last year at Thanksgiving, you were here with me;
We were not able to celebrate.
We spent Thanksgiving alone,
I don't remember what we ate.

You were not able to travel,
The kids had their own plans;
We spent Thanksgiving together,
Not knowing, it was the last we would spend.

Then Christmas time was nearing
And the memory is hard to bear,
You were getting ready to leave me,
You needed more than my care.

God saw you were tired and weary,
He knew you had suffered enough.
He said, "When this year is ended,
You will feel my delivering touch."

On the last day of the year, you left me,
But you did not go alone;
God sent His angels to bring you
To Himself, and to your Heavenly home.

So, this Thanksgiving, though I am lonely,
And I would love to spend it with you;
I give thanks to God you are with Him—
I will see you when my life is through.

November 23, 2024

CHRISTMAS LETTER TO ROBERT

I don't want to celebrate Christmas,
I don't want lights on a tree,
I don't want presents and tinsel,
All I want is you here with me.

Now Christmas only brings memories
Of watching you fade away.
I stood by your bed in the hospital,
My heart begging you to stay.

I knew you would soon be leaving,
Your life and your health were gone;
I did not want you to suffer,
But I never felt so alone.

For so many years we were together,
I never thought of being alone.
I knew if you had to leave me,
Our house would never be home.

But God had a different decision
He knew what you needed best;
He knew you were too sick to stay here,
So, He took you to Heaven's rest.

Last Christmas was nothing but heartache,
I watched as you slipped away.
This Christmas, for you, will be glorious,
With Christ, you will spend Christmas Day.

November 23, 2024

IF ROBERT COULD ANSWER FROM HEAVEN

You don't want to celebrate Christmas?
You don't want lights on a tree?
You would have to have glorified eyesight
To see the Light of God's Glory I see!

You won't remember the dying,
The hospital days are no more;
No heartbreaks or tears are allowed,
Only happiness and peace evermore.

You didn't want me to leave you;
I had many years on earth.
We had a long life together,
God decided that I should go first.

The years we had together
Seem long from your point of view;
But when you meet me in Heaven,
Eternity will never be through.

I didn't leave you by choice,
Our lives are in God's hands.
When my appointed days were over,
I went with the angel band.

For you, Christmas may have sad memories,
But look up, for the Day Star appears.
Tell our children and all my loved ones
I am waiting for you right here.

November 24, 2024

THANKSGIVING LUNCH

I ate Thanksgiving lunch with Sheila;
Lindsey and Jordan were there.
The grandkids had grown so much,
They are a delightful pair.

But I felt so empty and lonely—
My first Thanksgiving without you.
With you not seated beside me,
I was glad when the meal was through.

They are so kind and sweet to me;
They try to make me feel glad.
I love them for how they are trying,
But inside, I am so empty and sad.

I know I cannot be with you,
I know you cannot return.
But my heart feels like it is bursting,
For your presence and love, I so yearn.

I know you are dwelling in Heaven,
I know you are happy and free.
You may never think about me,
I don't know how Heaven will be.

I am trying to remember the good times,
To think of the life we had.
You were so precious to me,
I know I should not be sad.

Thanksgiving and Christmas were special,
They were days filled with joy from above.
I just hope you know up in Heaven
How deep for you, still, is my love.

November 28, 2024

December

And ye now therefore have sorrow:
but I will see you again,
and your heart shall rejoice,
and your joy no man taketh from you.

John 16:22

FINAL DAYS

Last year, on the first of December,
I didn't know when the month was through,
That you would forever leave me,
And I would say goodbye to you.

I knew you were getting weaker,
I knew your strength was gone,
But didn't think you would leave me,
I thought, somehow, you would hang on.

It would have been selfish to ask you
To stay, for you were so weak,
But to say goodbye to you--
These were words I never wanted to speak.

I am glad God didn't tell me
When your final day would come,
Or when you actually would go
To see your Heavenly home.

This Christmas I will miss you,
My heart is still so full of pain;
But I know one day in the future,
I will see you again.

My mind cannot grasp Heaven
Or what our relationship will be,
But I am assured with no doubt
I know you will welcome me.

December 1, 2024

GRIEF

We are in the month of December;
It is the month you went away.
It has been almost a year, and I miss you more each day.

A year without you—a year I've spent alone;
A year of heartache and sorrow,
A year I never wanted to come.

Life holds no joy without you;
Our home and my arms are bare.
My world is dark and empty without you here to share.

We did everything together; we didn't want to be apart.
I feel so hollow inside,
There's a hole where I once had a heart.

I thought as time passed I would feel better,
But the grief is stronger each day.
My heartbreak is new every morning,
I am so lonely since you went away.

No matter where I go or what I do,
Everything I see holds a memory of you.
If I am out for a drive or in a store,
It reminds me of you, and our life before.

I know you are happy, I know you are free
I am glad you have been delivered
From life's sufferings, you are free.

I long for the day I see you again,
When my life is over, and Eternity begins.
I don't know in Heaven how our life will be,
But I look forward to the day your sweet face I can see.

December 4, 2024

HOLIDAYS

I don't like this time of the year,
For in my heart, there is no cheer.
It was the time you went away,
I don't look forward to the Holidays.

Holiday means joy and fun,
But there's no joy in just being one.
Holidays are meant to be shared,
Not being alone, with no loved one there.

Holidays are hollow days,
I hear no songs of mirth.
My heart is sad, no joy I find,
Since you have left this earth.

I know I have to carry on,
But it's so hard since you are gone.
My smile is fake, it's all pretend,
With you not here my days to spend.

I know you'd say, "Don't be sad,
Just give thanks for the time we had.
It won't be long till your life is through;
I am waiting in Heaven to welcome you."

December 6, 2024

CHRISTMAS WEEK

It is the week before Christmas
And I am thinking of a year ago,
You were getting ready to leave me
I didn't know it would hurt so.
A year has passed without you,
I have never been so sad and blue;
I know you are happy in Heaven,
But I don't like life without you.

No Christmas lights are shining,
No Christmas tree is here;
I don't want to decorate,
It's not Christmas without you.

I try to go out and stay busy,
I go places and meet my friends,
Then I come home to a house so empty,
And my heart starts breaking again.

We had a long life together,
I know I should not complain,
But my arms are aching to hold you,
My heart is so full of pain.

I can't stop the tears from falling,
I can't keep you out of my mind,
No matter what I am involved in,
It's your face before me, I find.
I will never be happy without you,
My life will never be complete.
I know you are waiting in Heaven,
And I long for the time we will meet.

December 19, 2024

OUR LAST DAY

We didn't know one year ago
That we were spending our last day,
That when tomorrow's sun arose,
You would forever go away.

We did not know another night we would not spend
Or another meal we'd share;
We did not know that God would see,
You needed more than earth's care.

The hardest day I ever spent
was December twenty-third,
I never knew what silence was
Until your voice was not heard.

December twenty-second, you were so tired and ill;
Your health was gone, no cure was found,
In doctors or in pills.
God knew your time was over,
He had given you many days,
But I was still not ready to see you go away.

God said, "When this year is over,
I will take you home with Me,"
And December thirty-first, He set your spirit free.

I can't imagine what you have seen,
I know you are complete and whole,
To walk and run forever
on streets paved with pure gold.

Never again will you know pain,
No spending your days in a chair;
No doctors to see, you are forever free
No sickness or heartaches to bear.

December twenty-third was the day
They took you away,
And in just a week, you heard Jesus speak,
As He welcomed you home to stay.

Now I am left without you,
With broken heart and grief,
But I console myself in knowing,
That soon, again, we will meet.

December 22, 2024

DECEMBER TWENTY-THIRD

A year ago today
The ambulance came for you.
My heart broke in a thousand pieces,
For I knew your life would soon be through.

I don't know why you asked me to call them,
You knew you needed help;
I could not go with the ambulance,
You left here by yourself.

You knew when you were leaving
You would not come home again,
Your eyes were filled with tears
As you looked back, once again.

We followed you to the hospital
But the words you said were few.
I couldn't say what my heart felt,
For I knew I was losing you.

It has been so hard without you,
Life is just not right with you gone;
More than sixty years we were together,
I never thought of being alone.

I thank you for all that you gave me,
I thank you for your love so true,
I would give all that I own, and then some,
If I could spend Christmas with you.

December 23, 2024

MY SADDEST YEAR

No matter how long I live
Or how long my life will last,
I will never face another year
As sad as the one just passed.

There could ever be another day
That would hurt like losing you;
So no matter what the future holds,
My hardest day is through.

The last day of two thousand twenty-three
Was a day I hoped would never be.
It was the day you left this life,
I am now a widow, no longer a wife.

The year two thousand twenty-four
Was the hardest I ever faced,
Long lonely days and tear-filled nights,
I didn't know how one's heart could break.

So no matter what the rest of my life will be,
It will not be as bad as two thousand twenty-three.
For nothing could ever break my heart so,
As the year ended, I watched you go.

December 28, 2024

NEW YEAR'S EVE

New Year's Eve Two Thousand Twenty-Three
Brought a day I never wanted to be.
It was the day you left to go through Heaven's door,
Left me to walk alone thru Two Thousand Twenty-Four.

Now Two Thousand Twenty-Four is a memory too
Of three hundred sixty-six days of missing you.
I walked thru days of such deep sorrow,
Dreading each day to see another tomorrow.

I thought each day would never end
Long lonely nights that seemed without end.
Each morning I awoke to a house so still
Trying to find ways, the hours to fill.

Now the year is over, and I did make it through
Because Jesus said, "I will never leave you."
His promise He kept, for His word He keeps;
He comforts my heart, He sees when I weep.

So I will begin Two Thousand Twenty-Five
Assured more than ever, I know you are alive.
Never again will you suffer or die,
You are safe in Heaven under God's watchful eye.

So this coming year I will try to be strong
Even though for your presence, I know I will long.
There will never be a day I won't miss you
In this coming year, God will see me through.

December 31, 2024

YOUR HOMECOMING EVE

It was New Year's Eve when you went away,
Here's what the dictionary has to say.
"Eve" is the evening or day before
A special day, not experienced before.

God chose a special time for you to leave
Before "Eternal Day" it was your "Eve."
You finished the year, a soldier true,
God said, "Look what I have waiting for you."

He knew those you left would surely grieve
But it was your time, your special Eve.
The day you had anticipated was nearly in view,
For on New Year's Eve, this life was through.

We miss you so, and want you here,
Our hearts are empty, our eyes have tears.
But we are glad you are "home" to stay,
Last New Year's Eve was your homecoming day.

December 31, 2024

A LOOK BACK

A year ago today was your funeral;
I hardly knew I was there.
To see your body in a casket,
Was more heartache than I could bear.

I could not believe you had left me
I tried to pretend it wasn't true;
For the thought of facing life alone
I could not exist without you.

Now a year has gone by without you,
The saddest I ever lived,
I don't wish you back to suffer,
But to be with you, oh, what I would give.

We had a long life together,
But it would never be enough.
My real happiness and joy
Was found in your tender touch.

I thank God for the years He gave us.
I thank Him for the long life you had,
But I know in the year that lies before us
My heart will still be empty and sad.

I long for the time I see you
In Heaven, where I know you are,
And the love we shared on earth
In Eternity, will be better by far.

January 4, 2025

GOD IS, SO ALL IS WELL

No matter how lonely the day,
No matter how dark your lot,
May we never forget what God has said,
"I am God, and I change not."

So if God is, and we know it is true
Then why should we be cast down and blue?
When it seems the sun is covered in veil,
We know GOD IS, SO ALL IS WELL.

When we feel that God is nowhere near,
We can hear Him say, "I am right here.
I am so close, I have covered My face,
You couldn't bear to look on such Light and Grace."

So, when it seems we are all alone,
God still reigns on His mighty throne.
In the Light of His Glory, He continually dwells;
We know GOD IS, SO ALL IS WELL.

About the Author

Judy Proffitt writes from a lifetime of experiences and her deep personal faith in Jesus. Her words bring hope and joy, leading the reader into a spirit of grateful worship and awe for our Creator and Heavenly Father.

Judy still lives in the mountains of Western North Carolina, where she and her late husband, Robert, have deep roots. She enjoys reading, baking, and staying connected with her many friends and neighbors through encouraging notes and phone calls. Additionally, she is a devoted prayer warrior.

With her wit and wisdom, she continues to build a legacy of faith and love for her two children and their spouses, four grandchildren, and five great-grandchildren.

Robert and Judy with their five great-grandchildren.
(June 2023)